MW00423399

Published and distributed .... by ....
Group, LLC: www.neurobusinessgroup.com

Edited by Bonnie Egan and Kathy Glass

Library of Congress Cataloging-in-Publication Data

Printed in Cambridge, MA, USA

ISBN-13:
978-0615430720 (NeuroBusiness Group)
ISBN-10:
0615430724

The Science Behind
The Law of Attraction

A Step-by-Step Guide to Putting the Brain Science
Behind the Law of Attraction to Work for You©

Contents

Why use this workbook?

You've probably heard of the "Law of Attraction" and are either a fervent believer or think it's a load of hogwash. Regardless of your stance, have you had it work for you and do you understand why it works? If you have had the good fortune of being its beneficiary, the science behind it will be utterly fascinating. If you believe but are still waiting to attract that special someone, this brief and practical workbook will demonstrate how you can put the law of attraction to work. And for those of you who believe this is hogwash, I invite you to consider the science presented in these pages so that you can enhance your belief in a principle that will undoubtedly lead you to greater happiness if you apply yourself with full intensity.

In this debut and special edition, you may be inspired to use this book to help you think of this law in terms of your New Year's Resolution. If you are one of those who gets excited about making a New Year's Resolution and then find yourself in a puddle of melted dreams by midyear, you are not alone. Year after year people look forward to the New Year but have tremendous trouble keeping their minds on track. Let's take some classic situations:

WEIGHT LOSS: You know that 2011 is the year for weight loss and for taking these goals seriously. Get to the gym. Start that diet. Get back into those sexy jeans. So all you have to do is wait for the New Year to come around, and you'll be there. But wait! Haven't you already tried this? Wasn't 2010 supposed to be the year of the bikini— at least your bikini? Will 2011 be another dash of your bikini hopes?

GETTING MARRIED: Ah, yes. This year you joined two dating sites, actually went on a couple of awful dates, found yourself alone on the couch eating popcorn and watching reruns of *Law and Order*. What went wrong? Are you going to do the same thing again in 2011?

MAKING MORE MONEY: Yeah, right! Boy, did that train go the wrong way. Not only did you not make more money, you made less. And your workload increased. How did that happen?

BEING HAPPIER AND LESS STRESSED: A noble goal no doubt, but you might as well have tried to eat your soup with a knife and fork. No matter how hard you tried, it just wasn't happening.

THE INFAMOUS NEST EGG: That 401K you so diligently worked to build-that bastion of hope and security-lasted as long as a snowball in spring. Gone! Kaput! No more to be found. But 2010 was supposed to be the year to optimize this.

I could go on and on, and the reality is that 2011 is not going to be any better if you don't DO SOMETHING ABOUT IT! Sounds great, but what? You've already tried sticking to a strict schedule. You've already tried to imagine almost precisely what you want, but somehow the law of attraction never came into play.

Or did it? Perhaps it didn't work because you didn't know how to make it work. Is this just bogus, or is there some clear-cut science behind what you can do to make realization of your resolutions more likely?

In this workbook, you will find a science-based guide with references to seven concrete steps to take to optimize your brain so that you can make your New Year's Resolutions come to fruition. If you follow this guide closely, you will without a doubt increase your chances for the life of your dreams in 2011. Lots of folks out there made more money, someone out there got married this year, and someone out there lost weight. Why not you?

So read through each of the brain concepts. Make sure you understand what they mean, and then use the guide in each section to turn your aspirations into action. You are only seven steps away from getting to action. Why let 2011 be like 2010? And why rely on somewhat tired inspiration when science can offer you the answers that you have been looking for? Yes, science *can* help you reach your goals in a way that you've never tried before. Once you take possession of these seven principles, you can put these concepts to practice to remake your life.

Law # 1

There is a Right and a Wrong Way to Talk to Your Unconscious Brain

The Science

Have you ever wondered why it is that you often get the very opposite of what you want? Not only do you not get what you want, but the very thing you most feared comes your way. I first noticed this when people who had experienced panic attacks would be in a constant state of waiting for the next one— and sure enough, it came. And when it did, boy, was that uncomfortable! When I talk to people who have tried to lose weight, many report that they actually put on a few pounds, and when I talk to people who have worked much harder to deal with their economic worries, they observe that before they know it they have less money than when they worked half as hard.

Why is this and what can you do about it? The basis of this phenomenon is called "ironic process theory." This theory states that when you want something to NOT happen, it is more likely TO happen. How can this be?

In a recent article in the journal *Science* [1], psychologist Daniel Wegner explained that under stress, the brain behaves differently than it does when it is not under stress. Under ordinary circumstances, we are fortunate to have the lights turned on in the conscious and unconscious brain. The conscious brain is "upstairs" in the skull, and for all intents and purposes, the unconscious brain is "downstairs." However, under situations of stress, the light in the conscious brain is turned off and only the unconscious brain is working.

The problem is that the unconscious brain is quick to respond, but often inaccurate. It is the reflex part of the brain. So, say you are at a party, and you are carrying a glass of red wine and a cosmo back to your table, and there is a beautiful white couch on the way. You are carefully balancing the drinks (causing the stress) but as you get near the couch, your hands start to shake and before you know it, the beautiful hostess of the party cries out and the white couch is covered in wine and cranberry-flavored vodka. What exactly happened? You were careful to tell yourself NOT to do this, but the very thing you most dreaded happened. Why?

According to scientists who study this phenomenon, when you tell your brain NOT to do something under stress, it does not hear the word NOT. It simply hears what follows NOT. So when you say "DO NOT" drop the wine and cosmo, it only hears "DROP the wine and cosmo" and obeys you. This occurs despite trying to suppress the fear that you will drop the drinks.

That is because your unconscious brain searches for the thing you fear and tries to avoid it. If it is an unwanted thought, it keeps it out of your way. But under mental strain, controlling unwanted thoughts is not helpful, and a recent study has shown that when you let go of the fear of having to control them, you do much better. [2]

Part of what is happening is that in any given situation, when you have a goal there is always a warning-goal lurking in your mind. "Lose weight" may be the loudest voice in your head, but there is also a background voice of "don't snack." "Make more money" is always accompanied by the brain needing to suppress its spending (the background voice is "don't spend"), and doing the right thing on a date is always accompanied by that background voice saying: "whatever you do, do NOT mention your ex." These things happen in the brain at the same time. The "dos" may be your louder voice, but the unconscious brain also works to suppress the "don'ts."

Usually, the "don'ts" are there to help prevent dreaded outcomes. Your unconscious searches for these goals to make sure they do not happen. But when the conflict center of the brain is overloaded, as it is during times of stress, it fails to suppress this information, and in its search for the goal you want to prevent, the very thing you want to prevent happens. It is as though stress takes away the power of the unconscious to keep what you dread away from the situation, and all of a sudden you are snacking, spending, or mentioning your ex. "Don't" is a fence that keeps unwanted things out, but under stress, that fence breaks down. Why is this?

The reason is a phenomenon known as "cognitive priming." Multiple studies have demonstrated this phenomenon. For example, when people are asked NOT to think about a forbidden word, under stress they can't help doing so. [3] Also, when people are asked NOT to think about a word and then asked to name colors, if the word is shown to them while they are seeing a color, they name the color more slowly. [3, 4] For each instance, when under stress we can see that what is forbidden interferes with the task at hand. It either slows the task down or the person fails to suppress the forbidden thought or action. A classic example is when you ask people to think of as many animals as they can in one minute but you add "DO NOT think about a white bear." Inevitably, they do.

If these laboratory experiments do not convince you of this, consider the phenomenon of "yips." Yips are sudden, often jerky movements— literal body movements— that occur when you do not intend them to occur. They have been described in major-league baseball players (Steve Blass and Rick Ankiel) and also in golf, specifically while putting. In fact, Ankiel called his sudden involuntary movement "The Creature." Soccer players, too, if told to NOT kick the ball to a certain part of the goal when trying to score a penalty goal, look exactly where they are asked not to look. [1] It is as if your brain is tempted for perverse reasons.

One of the areas in life where this can cause some trouble is when you are trying not to think of a forbidden romance. Studies show that trying not to think about a forbidden romance makes you think of exactly this when under stress. [5, 6] If you are at a party and have a crush on someone and try to hard to suppress this in front of your current partner, it ramps up the desire to have an affair. Or if you tell yourself not to date someone at work, under stress that very thing could happen.

When your unconscious has to control negative worries under stress, it gives up control and these worries become manifest. Stress removes the "do not" in that it removes the ability to suppress the unwanted behavior or thought. Stress is the ultimate fence remover.

Thus we can see that stress is a saboteur that prevents the unconscious from suppressing what it needs to. Instead, the very thing you do not desire is manifested. Stress, in effect, changes the polarity of your magnet to start to attract the opposite of what you want.

The Solutions

Based on this research, what are some of the steps you can take? What can you consider to reverse the polarity of your mind and counter the unconscious? Or how can you work with your unconscious as you are trying to manifest your goals?

1. Avoid "do not" when you are thinking of getting what you want. Provide self-instructions in the "do" form. For example, if going out on a date, talk to yourself about what you want to do rather than what you want to not do.

2. Lessen the amount of mental control of unwanted ideas when under stress. For example, if you are worried about spending money, think more about saving than not spending.

3. If you find yourself prone to "jerky" or "out of control" self-sabotage, know that this is deeply connected with too much stress and undertake to decrease your stress before you try something out. Too much impulsive sex? Too many anger outbursts? Think of the stress fence remover and do something about it. For example, take a yoga class or do some meditation or go for a walk to cool down.

Exercises

AVOIDING "DO NOT"

1. Write down three resolutions or goals that you have:

....

....

....

....

....

....

2. Write down three things you would like to avoid
related to each goal:

Goal 1:

....

Three Things to Avoid:

....

....

....

....

....

....

Goal 2:

....

Three Things to Avoid:

....

....

....

....

....

....

Goal 3:

....

Three Things to Avoid:

....

....

....

....

....

....

Now recognize what these three things are, and when you find yourself in the situation, remember them. If they occur to you as "do not" statements, convert them into "do" statements.

3. Rewrite each desire to avoid as a desire to do. For example, if you want to avoid snacking, write: "Find a way to surround myself with healthy snacks." Or if you want to avoid spending, write: "Find a way to make up a budget that I can stick to." Or if you want to avoid alienating someone, write: "Focus on these three ways to draw this person closer."

Goal 1:

....

Three Things to Avoid - Reframed:

....
....
....
....
....
....

Goal 2:

....

Three Things to Avoid - Reframed:

....

....

....

....

....

....

Goal 3:

....

Three Things to Avoid - Reframed:

....

....

....

....

....

....

Memorize these positive statements and look at them as often as you can— at least daily. This will begin to reprogram your mind.

LESSEN MENTAL CONTROL

When you find yourself trying to exclude negative thoughts, let go of the process altogether. Refocus your efforts on the positive frames mentioned above, or simply place your attention on where these negative thoughts are without analyzing or trying to think about them. (In Law #3 on stress and imagination, you will understand the science behind why this helps.) Essentially, then, resist the temptation to control negative thoughts when under stress. Simply do not engage them. From a purely scientific standpoint, things will be more likely to happen in the direction you want them to. Wayne Dyer's way of dealing with this is to say "Next." In Tai Chi they say that when your opponent comes at you with full force, instead of pushing them back, move out of the way. This will cause them to fall. It is the same with negative thoughts. Simply move out of the way. When speaking to a friend about this recently, I recalled the song by Snoop Dogg called "Drop It Like It's Hot." I think of all negative self-instructions as "hot"— so I drop them.

STOP AFTER THE FIRST OR SECOND REACTIVE MOMENT AND TAKE A BREAK

If you find yourself "messing up" in a reactive way (for example, saying the wrong thing or doing the opposite of what you want), turn your attention to your stress center and do something to decrease your stress before your next attempt. Going for a walk, meditating, exercising, breathing deeply, or participating in a yoga class can all be helpful before you return to the goal at hand.

Now you may ask, if this is so much work, how are you "attracting" anything? The answer is that you are increasing the power of your magnet to increase the force of attraction to what you want. This "work" is really about preparing your brain to be the magnet that it is. The unconscious brain will start to lead you to your goals much faster, and it will seek out the right steps much more effectively. But this is just the beginning. Read on to understand more about how to increase the power of your mind magnets.

Law # 2

Mental imagery is the blueprint
for the brain's action plans

The Science

We constantly hear that imagining what you want will help you get there, but is this really true? How does simply imagining put the law of attraction to work? Sports psychology stands out as the prime example of how imagery can be helpful. By imagining specific movement in sport, imagery can improve performance by enhancing the technical execution of movement as well as the intrinsic motivation of individuals. That's right: imagining moving can improve the way you feel and perform. [7] Expert athletes first imagine the record times they want to run in their races and then run their races in that exact time. In fact, simply imagining can actually improve flexibility of different muscle groups as well. [8] Imagery helps athletes become confident, and as a result, their performance ends up being superior. [9] It helps to prevent resignation. Studies have also shown that when we imagine moving, our eyes move as though we are actually moving, which indicates that our brains are similarly engaged in both tasks. [10] But do we actually know this?

It turns out that imagining moving and actually moving both activate overlapping brain regions. [11] When we actually move, we activate additional brain regions, and the movement areas of the brain connect even more. But there is still considerable overlap between imagining areas and moving areas of the brain. The imagery warms up the action brain and works as a blueprint for action.

It is important to emphasize that mental imagery is not simply thinking about something; it is actually using effort to imagine the scene as if it were a movie in your head. Simply simulating (imitating or partially representing) a movement is not the same as actively imagining it, as these activities activate different brain regions. [12] Stop for a minute and think about this. First imitate someone giving a public speech. Now close your eyes and imagine yourself standing at a podium in front of a room filled with people listening to you speak. They are entirely different experiences!

As the other laws will show you, simply imagining is not enough, but it definitely warms up the action brain to start acting. [13] This "start" can get the process going and improve accuracy and performance. [14]

So what does this have to do with the law of attraction? The law of attraction says that you get what you put out. When you put out goal-directed images of what you want, the brain activates to start to take you there. Images are a powerful stimulator of automatic action and transcend merely talking about what you want or partially reading or thinking about it. They are one of the closest steps to action and also give the action-brain information about where it needs to go. You can think of them as maps or blueprints that the action brain refers to when trying to reach its goals.

In sports psychology, we know that the time course of imagined actions parallels the actual time taken to act. Thus, when we imagine, if we imagine the actual time taken to do something, we may be more likely to reproduce this in real life. [15-17]

Note the following about imagery:
1. The goal is known.

2. In many cases, the process is not known or guaranteed; it is imagined. It is a "story" about breaking a record. You do not need proof of reality to imagine.

3. The imagery has to be practiced. It is not a one-time exercise.

4. Your ability to imagine movement can improve over time. Measure this ability and see if you can improve on it.

5. Imagine your goals in a quiet place since distractions will interrupt your imagination's focus.

To put imagery into practice to increase the potential to attract what you want to yourself, follow the instructions in the solutions.

The Solutions

Start to improve your imagination process using the following practice guide regularly for six weeks. If you could do this at least once a day, you will significantly warm up your action brain both consciously and unconsciously. This is the architectural process of initiating your blueprints.

Imagine three things that you want in the New Year, e.g. more money, more happiness, to get married, or better health. Really imagine them— as a movie with a story rather than a static image.

Exercises

1. Write down three goals for the upcoming year.

....

....

....

....

....

....

2. Write down how each goal will be "discovered." For example, you will be standing on a scale and the weight will read...or you will be looking at an ATM and...

....

....

....

....

....

....

3. Now spend five minutes imagining each of the three discovery points above. Note any details below after imagining with your eyes closed.

....

....

....

....

....

....

For each discovery point, fill in the circles below as steps that precede and lead to it.

Goal 1:

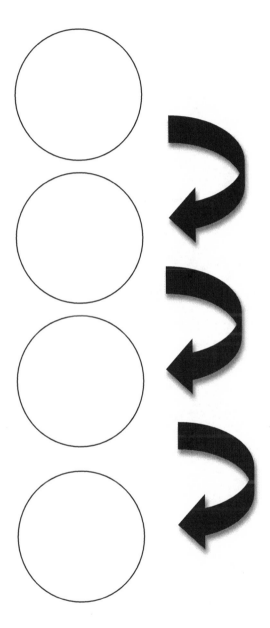

Goal 2:

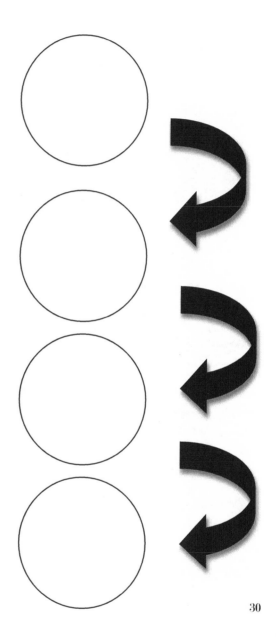

Goal 3:

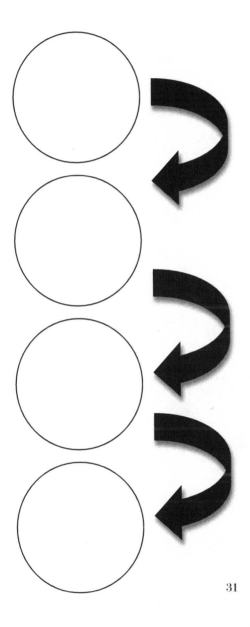

5. Now take five minutes for each goal and imagine the steps that precede it. Literally imagine them. If you feel impatient, take a break and come back to this.

Use the grid below for each day of the week for six weeks to check off your accomplishment of this step:

Week 1	Day 1	Day 2	Day 3	Day 4	Day 5	Day 6	Day 7
Imagine in color							
Imagine in Motion							
Imagine in detail							

Week 2	Day 1	Day 2	Day 3	Day 4	Day 5	Day 6	Day 7
Imagine in color							
Imagine in Motion							
Imagine in detail							

Week 3	Day 1	Day 2	Day 3	Day 4	Day 5	Day 6	Day 7
Imagine in color							
Imagine in Motion							
Imagine in detail							

Week 4	Day 1	Day 2	Day 3	Day 4	Day 5	Day 6	Day 7
Imagine in color							
Imagine in Motion							
Imagine in detail							

Week 5	Day 1	Day 2	Day 3	Day 4	Day 5	Day 6	Day 7
Imagine in color							
Imagine in Motion							
Imagine in detail							

Week 6	Day 1	Day 2	Day 3	Day 4	Day 5	Day 6	Day 7
Imagine in color							
Imagine in Motion							
Imagine in detail							

Law # 3

Subtle differences in how you imagine can make all the difference to the brain

The Science

So far, you have understood how to think (in a positive frame) and how imagination warms up the action center of the brain. However, imagination by itself is not the most that you can do. Aside from imagining in color, in motion, and in a quiet place, there are several characteristics that can optimize the way you imagine. In Law #3, we will look at imagining in the first and third person.

So what exactly does imagining in the first person mean? If you were planning to run a race, and I asked you to imagine doing this, you might imagine the following: you are on the track, wearing white shorts, your hair is blowing in the wind, and your eyes are focused on the finish line. This, however, is you in the third person. That is, you are looking at yourself rather than being in the race. To actually be in the race, you have to train your brain to not see your own eyes. Instead, you are actually on the track, and all you can see is the track ahead and the finish line. You are not looking at yourself. You have to put yourself in that position. We call this attitude of being in the first person "embodied" imagery because your entire body feels as though it is in your goal. Take a minute to practice this. First focus, then put yourself on that track.

Or if, for example, you are thinking of losing weight, when you imagine standing on the scale, you do not see yourself; all you see is your feet on the scale and the needle that moves as you stand on it. You are excited as you see the needle move to the lower weight, or as you see the flashes before the digital number shows. If you want to make money, imagine yourself looking at the screen of the ATM with a sense of excitement pulsing through your body.

What happens when you imagine actually doing something? When you imagine, it sends information to your brain that becomes a plan. We call these "motor plans." [18] Motor plans allow your brain to make the right choices about where it wants to look and where it wants to go. You attract the right opportunities, because now your brain knows where to look and is ultra-sensitive to subtle information. As a result, you will pick up relevant information because the image is something the brain can hold onto, especially if in the first person. When you imagine the steps in the first person, you will find that your action center will also warm up more than if you imagine in the third person.

How do we know this? A recent study has shown that first-person imagery or embodied imagery (where you are totally in the situation you imagine) is much more powerful in stimulating the brain's action center than third-person imagery [19, 20]. Both first- and third-person imagery stimulate the planning centers for movement [21], but first-person perspectives are more powerful stimulators. Brain imaging studies teach us that this imagery activates overlapping areas in the brain, but that there are also distinct regions that are specific to each [22]. The brain can distinguish between an action performed by you or someone else. However, third-person imagery may also be effective, and being able to switch between both can be helpful to the strength of the image in your brain [22]. Athletes use this technique to improve performance. First they watch other people doing what they are supposed to do, and then they try to develop a strong image of themselves doing it [23].

Furthermore, another interesting study found that the action center of the brain does not activate when you watch a moving dot, but it does activate when you search for patterns on the moving dot [24, 25]. Thus, it is not helpful to simply imagine or watch yourself acting without involving yourself by asking questions or searching for details of your actions. Instead, when you imagine what you want, look for patterns in your own actions or thoughts, and be engaged in what you are imagining. As you make your image clearer, you are also making it a more effective motor plan or motor map [26].

So what if the activation is stronger for first-person imagery? The stronger the image, the clearer it is. The clearer the image, the more effective it is [26] since greater clarity activates the brain more [27].

This "clarity" refers to more than just imagining; it also refers to every sense that you use to imagine. The smell of the gym, the joy of seeing your bank balance rise, the taste of bread in your new kitchen— the more clearly you can imagine things like this, the stronger your action brain will activate. People often think that they are imagining when they are not. True imagination requires intense focus and commitment.

Thus, in order to warm up the action center in your brain to become more sensitive to subtle cues that will guide you toward your goal, imagining in the first person (in an embodied way) provides helpful plans to your brain. This is in addition to imagining in the third person, which (like in the example of athletes mentioned above) may be an effective place to start.

The Solutions

To fully enhance your imagination skills, the following tips are useful:

1. First, observe someone else who has done what you want to do.
2. Then, imagine that person getting to the goal.
3. Now, imagine yourself getting to the goal.
4. Imagine not just what you are doing, but how you are feeling.
5. Add as many senses as you can to your imagination.
6. When watching yourself move toward your goal, do not simply watch. Literally watch and look for

patterns in your old responses and establish new patterns that will help you.

Below is an abbreviated example of how you can do this:

If your goal is to buy a house:

1. Identify one person in a similar situation who has done this. You can also use a website like http://michaelbluejay.com/house/howmuchhome.html or http://www.wikihow.com/Buy-a-House.

2. Then, close your eyes and memorize the steps that someone else would go through to get to this goal.

3. Now, imagine how you would get to this goal using similar steps. Imagine, for example, being in the situation of making more money.

4. Imagine how you will feel as you move through these steps.

5. Now imagine things to involve other senses: the sight of money, the smell of fresh paint, the texture of a smooth wood floor, etc.

6. Identify old patterns that kept you stuck, and now imagine new patterns that will get you unstuck.

Remember, these are not simply "magical" steps that somehow draw what you want into your life; they convey important information to your brain that helps the brain follow subtle cues when it comes across them.

If you repeat these steps, they will refine your imagination.

Exercises

Take the same three goals you identified earlier and apply each of these steps to those goals over six weeks. Use the grid below to check off whether you applied yourself to these goals.

Goal 1:

....

....

....

....

....

....

Week 1	Day 1	Day 2	Day 3	Day 4	Day 5	Day 6	Day 7
Observe another person							

Imagine another person							
Imagine yourself							
Add feelings							
Add other senses							
Identify old patterns							

Week 2	Day 1	Day 2	Day 3	Day 4	Day 5	Day 6	Day 7
Observe another person							
Imagine another person							
Imagine yourself							
Add feelings							
Add other senses							
Identify old patterns							

Week 3	Day 1	Day 2	Day 3	Day 4	Day 5	Day 6	Day 7
Observe another person							
Imagine another person							
Imagine yourself							
Add feelings							
Add other senses							
Identify old patterns							

Week 4	Day 1	Day 2	Day 3	Day 4	Day 5	Day 6	Day 7
Observe another person							
Imagine another person							
Imagine yourself							
Add feelings							
Add other senses							
Identify old patterns							

Week 5	Day 1	Day 2	Day 3	Day 4	Day 5	Day 6	Day 7
Observe another person							
Imagine another person							
Imagine yourself							
Add feelings							
Add other senses							
Identify old patterns							

Week 6	Day 1	Day 2	Day 3	Day 4	Day 5	Day 6	Day 7
Observe another person							
Imagine another person							
Imagine yourself							
Add							

feelings							
Add other senses							
Identify old patterns							

Goal 2:

....

....

....

....

....

....

Week 1	Day 1	Day 2	Day 3	Day 4	Day 5	Day 6	Day 7
Observe another person							
Imagine another person							
Imagine yourself							
Add feelings							
Add other senses							
Identify old patterns							

Week 2	Day 1	Day 2	Day 3	Day 4	Day 5	Day 6	Day 7
Observe another person							
Imagine another							

person							
Imagine yourself							
Add feelings							
Add other senses							
Identify old patterns							

Week 3	Day 1	Day 2	Day 3	Day 4	Day 5	Day 6	Day 7
Observe another person							
Imagine another person							
Imagine yourself							
Add feelings							
Add other senses							
Identify old patterns							

Week 4	Day 1	Day 2	Day 3	Day 4	Day 5	Day 6	Day 7
Observe another person							
Imagine another person							
Imagine yourself							
Add feelings							
Add other senses							
Identify old patterns							

Week 5	Day 1	Day 2	Day 3	Day 4	Day 5	Day 6	Day 7
Observe another person							
Imagine another person							
Imagine yourself							
Add feelings							
Add other senses							
Identify old patterns							

Week 6	Day 1	Day 2	Day 3	Day 4	Day 5	Day 6	Day 7
Observe another person							
Imagine another person							
Imagine yourself							
Add feelings							
Add other senses							
Identify old patterns							

Goal 3:

....

....

....

....

....

....

Week 1	Day 1	Day 2	Day 3	Day 4	Day 5	Day 6	Day 7
Observe another person							
Imagine another person							
Imagine yourself							
Add feelings							
Add other senses							
Identify old patterns							

Week 2	Day 1	Day 2	Day 3	Day 4	Day 5	Day 6	Day 7
Observe another person							
Imagine another person							
Imagine yourself							
Add feelings							
Add other senses							
Identify old patterns							

Week 3	Day 1	Day 2	Day 3	Day 4	Day 5	Day 6	Day 7
Observe another person							
Imagine another							

47

person							
Imagine yourself							
Add feelings							
Add other senses							
Identify old patterns							

Week 4	Day 1	Day 2	Day 3	Day 4	Day 5	Day 6	Day 7
Observe another person							
Imagine another person							
Imagine yourself							
Add feelings							
Add other senses							
Identify old patterns							

Week 5	Day 1	Day 2	Day 3	Day 4	Day 5	Day 6	Day 7
Observe another person							
Imagine another person							
Imagine yourself							
Add feelings							
Add other senses							
Identify old patterns							

Week 6	Day 1	Day 2	Day 3	Day 4	Day 5	Day 6	Day 7
Observe another person							
Imagine another person							
Imagine yourself							
Add feelings							
Add other senses							
Identify old patterns							

Law # 4

Reframing impossible wishes clears the brain pathways for action

The Science

When we want to attract things to our lives, we are often deterred by the seeming impossibility. As a result, we tell our brains that something is not possible and simply stop them from finding the solutions we seek. If something seems impossible, we imagine that it is, but this lowers the chances that we will ever get there.

If you doubt this for a minute, simply think of the example of Roger Bannister, who is credited with the unique distinction of breaking the record for the four-minute mile. Before him, nobody could do this. Prior to breaking this record, he had the realization that this was possible when he ran a race in 4:03.6. Once he was close enough, he started to believe that this was possible. Then on May 6, 1954, Bannister broke the record at 3 minutes, 59.4 seconds. This showed that once his brain computed that something was possible, it stretched to meet this demand. Another big lesson can be learned from the fact that in the year following Bannister's record-breaking run, several people broke this record: once people believed that something once deemed impossible was, in fact, possible, their brains organized the information to bring them to their goals. Believing is critical because it allows the brain to stay online to come up with answers. Once we stop believing, we ask the brain to turn off. This is the singular benefit of optimism.

I want to point out that this is different from blind faith. While faith is important, we must be prepared to *act into* this faith. Action is one of the cornerstones of attraction. It is what brings us close enough to our goals to finally believe with conviction. Even magnets "act" by pulling or pushing.

In the course of world history, many events once deemed impossible have been made possible: man has walked on the moon, flown an airplane, broken records for serve speeds in tennis...the list is endless. Only those who dare to imagine the impossible allow their brains to come up with solutions to find out how to get there. The purer this belief, the better it works.

The problem with how we think today is that we have become victims of probability. We use probability as a measure of reality— which it may well be. But it is not a measure of what is possible. Or what is exceptional.

Think of this for a minute: no world record would have been broken if nobody tried because they thought this was not likely. Imagine what would have happened if the Wright brothers listened to people when they decided to make something that could fly! Imagine what the naysayers said when somebody thought we could connect the whole world with the internet. Not very probable, but these dreams came true nonetheless.

So what does it mean when something seems impossible? What happens to the brain when we try to imagine something despite the fact that it is "impossible"? If we start with observation, we know that in stroke patients, observing others perform an action activates critical parts of their brains that stimulate recovery [28]. That is, simply by watching somebody move, his or her brain starts to want to move in the same way. The brain starts to understand that something is possible by imitating it at a lower level [29]. Even when people watch physically implausible movement, this type of observation stimulates the brain as much as watching plausible movement [30]. Taking this one step further, it has also been shown that when we imagine implausible movements (movements that are physically impossible such as rotating your hand 360 degrees), the brain still registers this as an action [31] in a way that is not remarkably different from imagining a movement that is possible and plausible.

Since we know that imagery causes movement planning (because it is a blueprint), stimulating the brain with impossible ideas, if we are patient enough, we will create movement plans that will guide us toward our goals. Along the way, we may make errors, but each error is a learning point about how and where to correct our navigation. Too many people stop at these errors, seeing such errors as a confirmation that what they first thought of as impossible is actually impossible instead of re-navigating their course toward the goal.

People often select ridiculous examples to try to refute the approach of attraction by believing. They may say: if I sit in this chair, a million dollars will fall in my lap, or if I just have faith, I will find a way to get married. True faith involves being willing to act into this belief. We are endowed with action centers in our brains. If we simply wish to be "given" things without acting, these things do not generally come. The real giving is in the solution. Once we figured out that it was possible to go to the moon, we still had to do it. Once we knew that it was possible to climb Mount Everest, we still had to do it. All billionaires have made their money by acting at some level. It is a shame when people believe that having faith means not acting when, in fact, research shows that having faith prepares the brain for action. The brain will figure out if something is implausible, and this something may be implausible, but general life goals are usually not implausible, even when we think they are.

At this point, you may say: if all this involves is trying, then why do I need to imagine or self-speak in a certain way? And here is the critical point: simple effort is not likely to take you where you want to go. The unconscious or unconscious brain can take you there much faster if you give it certain information. You may not know how it takes you there, but it will. Positive self-talk, imagery, embodied imagining, and now possibility thinking all give the unconscious brain the information it needs to seek a solution.

If we look at the usual comments that people make, we can provide rational examples of exceptions. Take a look at the examples below.

Argument	Exception or counter-argument
At my age, I am never going to find a life partner.	The oldest woman ever to get married was Minnie Munro, who married an 82-year-old man when she was 102 years old; at a less extreme level, many people do, in fact, get married when they are much older.
There is no way for me to become a billionaire.	Alfred Mann is a self-made billionaire who grew up poor and sold magazines and lemonade as a boy in Oregon. There are many other stories of people making it suddenly by pursuing their dreams.

If you look beyond these examples, you can generally be assured that there are at least a few people who have been in your position in life. How have they overcome their obstacles and adversities to achieve success? Having faith is one thing, but the idea is to act into that faith. Do not simply apply effort; use the power of these laws to give the best possible information to your brain to get where you want to get faster.

The Solutions

Therefore, if you have a goal that seems out of reach, decide what IS within reach and then build on that. If you divide any "out of reach" goal into "within reach" goals, you will see, every step along the way, that what you need to do to increase your chances of getting to the next stage will become more doable.

Exercises

For each of the goals identified earlier, write out a staged approach that represents a fraction of the goal. As you write this out, spend ten minutes a day imagining how you can get to the first goal. As a rule, make the first goal reachable. Remember that "reachable" may mean sacrifice, so prepare to change your current patterns of behavior. For example, your goal is to buy a house, and you need $10,000 more on an annual net salary of $40,000 in order to make a down payment and monthly mortgage payments. Your first step toward your goal is to decide how much more you can save per month than you are currently saving. If this amount is $400, then document it. Basically, rather than being overwhelmed by your goal, decide on the first reachable goal in the right direction.

Goal 1:

....

....

Stage 1:

....

....

Stage 2:

....

....

Stage 3:

....

....

Stage 4:

....

....

Stage 5:

....

....

Goal 2:

....

....

Stage 1:

....

....

Stage 2:

....

....

Stage 3:

....

....

Stage 4:

....

....

Stage 5:

....
....

Goal 3:

....
....

Stage 1:

....
....

Stage 2:

....
....

Stage 3:

....
....

Stage 4:

....
....

Stage 5:

....

....

Law # 5

Our brains act as automatic mirrors

The Science

The law of attraction says simply that likes attracts like. And while we may debate whether this is true or not, there is considerable scientific evidence to back up why this is, in fact, true. Essentially, this law states that if you are positive, what you want will come to you. Many refute this law because they think that either they are incapable of being positive or that positivity by itself does not deliver what you want. Yet there are now considerable examples from science about why this notion of attraction may have some truth to it.

First, the mirror neuron system is a system of brain nerve cells that act together to reflect whatever we are exposed to. If we see someone move in a certain way, this movement is represented in our own brains almost as though we are moving. That is, there is an automatic reflection in the mirror of an observer's brain [32, 33]. This mirroring can also occur when we infer intention from another person (that is, other people's intentions can automatically register in our brains) [34-36]. We can "sense" bad intentions. Similarly, this mirror neuron system also mirrors emotions automatically, so that before we know it, we are reflecting the emotions of others in the mirrors of our brains [37, 38].

Think of how often this happens when you come home in a good mood and your partner is in a bad mood. Within seconds, you start to "reflect" their bad mood and think it is your own.

Thus, when people react to us, they may be simply putting out what is being mirrored by their brains. It turns out that this mirroring may be more powerful for fear than for happiness [39]. Numerous studies have shown that when we are exposed to emotions, our brains may co-create "simulations" of these emotions [40-42]. Conversely, when we put out certain emotions, we "attract" those emotions right back to us.

Why is this significant and how does this substantiate the law of attraction? First, whatever emotion we put out, we "attract" to ourselves. If we put out happiness, we cause this to be formed in the mirror neurons of others and they become happy. If we put out fear, this also causes fear in others that comes back to us. Thus at this level, the attraction of the same emotion is inevitable.

This is interesting in many different situations. If you feel not loved enough and you put that out, you create a similar emotion in another person. You get back the emotions you put out. When you feel emotionally needy, this emotion is then reflected in the mirror neuron system in other people's brains, and they feel an emptiness that relates to need. In this case, self-satisfaction is important, as this will then lead other people to feel this emotion and want to be close to you. This leaves us with a difficult but inevitable truth: to get what we want emotionally, we cannot rely on others consistently. We have to pursue our own goals and this satisfaction will then draw out similar emotions in others. Since fear is a stronger emotion— in terms of creating a reflection in others— we have to be careful about this, since when we feel threatened, we can easily spread this emotion to people we come in contact with. Since this is the case, we are doomed to be lonely if we give in to the early emotions in a relationship. This is why like attracts like in terms of emotions.

However, another consequence of this is that emotions dictate where our attention goes. When we are fearful, this consumes attention and our attention is directed toward threatening or fearful things [43, 44]. This means that the way we see the world is through a fearful lens, and this lens then determines how we interpret life. If we always feel threatened or fearful, this determines how we experience life. In addition to "attracting" fear from others, when we are fearful we also tend to pay too much attention to fearful or threatening things. Our emotions instruct our attentional systems about where to look. If we are afraid, we are more likely to look for threatening things and miss out on the happier things or even solutions. If we are happier, there is a greater chance that we will not be biased to look out only for threat and will therefore "attract" solutions to ourselves. We let this go in our day-to-day lives because we are often stressed, but remember, the first stress makes you look for the second and so on. Stop the stress cycle when you notice how it starts to grow.

If we look more deeply at these phenomena, there is an almost illusory quality to "emotion." If we are governed by emotions, how we think about things is really determined by how we feel and not by what is actually happening. In the same situation, one person who is predisposed to being fearful and another who does not feel fear will experience the world in completely different ways. Each person will have a completely different way of thinking [45]. We attract what we want to our lives because we instruct our attention to look for things that support our emotional outlook. If we are fearful, we tell our attention to look for threatening things, and if we are happy, we see the positive things about life.

In the table below, we can see what we put out that is potentially mirrored in our brains or the brains of others:

Your own emotion	Consequences
I need to be rich.	People who could give you money feel: "I need" (as opposed to "I will give you").
I need to be married to you.	People who could marry you feel: "I feel anxious too" (as opposed to "I feel calm and happy and want to connect").

I feel pessimistic about my possibilities.	You tell your attention to only look for negative things (evolutionarily, we look out for threat to protect ourselves).
I am desperate for a house.	Your desperation eats up your attention so that you cannot think clearly about a creative strategy to get that house.
I am afraid that you will leave me.	People who could stay with you feel threatened as well and leave.

Another reality that many people are unaware of is that when we try to imagine or use imagery when worried, worry deactivates the very parts of the brain needed to mount an image [46]. As a result, we cannot sustain the positive image for long enough to create motor plans. Thus, worry "attracts" negative things in part because when we try to imagine positive things, the brain is unable to sustain this image.

The Solutions

The problem with being at the mercy of our emotions is that it means that we have to be consistently happy, which is almost impossible. However, we can catch ourselves when making estimations of the world while we are anxious or threatened and reframe what we see as being biased by our feelings. Some people are more positive than others, and positive emotions have been shown to lead to better decisions and greater success [47, 48]. Thus, if we can manage to change our emotions when pursuing our life goals to being more positive, we will be more likely to "attract" positive outcomes to our lives. Positive moods seem to create positive moods in others, and we are more likely to get what we want when we have these moods. We must remember that we cannot simply fake these moods unless we are doing so to eventually build toward the real emotion.

Another option is to transcend emotions. To do this, we can develop a more observational quality about any emotion and recognize that emotions affect how we solve our problems. Thus, instead of being a slave to our emotions, we focus on our efforts to get to our goals without desperation or fear.

In summary, the solutions here are:
1. Emotion-interrupt: interrupt your emotions in the midst of negative "landslides" and focus on positive things.

2. Focus on self-development.

3. Avoid worry when imagining positive outcomes.

4. Transcend emotions by recognizing how they are arbitrary brain activations.

5. Counter-mirror other people's negative emotions by recognizing that when you feel negative, you are simply taking on somebody else's negative emotions. You can recognize that this is happening and rather than automatically mirror their emotions, develop a habit of focusing on positive things.

Exercises

1. Develop a personal reminder list of positive things to focus on when you begin to worry. Each week, write out three positive things about your life, no matter how seemingly inconsequential. For example, "I am in good health"; "summer will come around again"; "massages make me feel better." Use the table below.

Week	Positive Reminders
One	1
	2
	3
Two	1
	2

	3	
Three	1	
	2	
	3	
Four	1	
	2	
	3	
Five	1	
	2	
	3	
Six	1	
	2	
	3	

2. Revisit the goals you set above and rewrite the staged approach to them in a state of non-worry and imagined excitement and positivity.

Goal 1:

....

....

Stage 1:

....

....

Stage 2:

....

....

Stage 3:

....

....

Stage 4:

....

....

Stage 5:

....

....

Goal 2:

....

....

Stage 1:

....

....

Stage 2:

....
....

Stage 3:

....,.................................
....

Stage 4:

....
....

Stage 5:

....
....

Goal 3:

....
....

Stage 1:

....
....

Stage 2:

....

....

Stage 3:

....

....

Stage 4:

....

....

Stage 5:

....

....

3. Play the mind-mirror game every morning for ten minutes using the following steps:

3.1. Identify one insecurity you have.

3.2. Imagine that need is fulfilled but you just can't see it.

3.3. Draw a picture of the mind mirror you want to take into your day with you. Below are some pictures to get you started. Notice how they don't need to be an artist's rendition but instead can be your own pictures that you draw.

Happiness

Contentment

Joyful
anticipation

Playfulness

Draw mirrors like this that you can call on during your
day and develop a library of positive mirrors. Use the
blank boxes below to draw your own mirrors to show to
the world.

Law # 6

The softer voices of our
unconscious brains are not
really softer; they are louder
but beyond our abilities to
hear

The Science

We tend to believe that the events and circumstances of our lives come to us because of conscious mental processes. We believe that we are in control of what we attract, but we are, in reality, in the grip of our unconscious brains. Therefore, the exercises of the past section are really useful if you practice them enough to reprogram your unconscious brain. As purely conscious tools, their use is limited. Why is that?

Several studies show that the decisions we make are often based on unconscious factors that we try to suppress. Unconscious voices are powerful and louder instructions than our conscious voices, but much like dog whistles, they are at a "frequency" that we cannot hear. One study showed that the seeds of relationship decay, for example, are sown long before people are aware of their feelings [49]. We "attract" negative outcomes because we cannot acknowledge our unacceptable feelings since they are threatening and unconscious. In fact, our overt feelings are not as reliable as the unconscious feelings in terms of predictors of the end of relationships [50].

The power of the unconscious is quite breathtaking. For example, if we subliminally influence a person's unconscious with statements that have to do with a prior secure relationship (so that they are not aware that you are doing this), they are more likely to be authentic in their current relationships [51]. You can prime them to feel more secure. The decisions we make on an everyday basis can also be influenced by our surroundings or former experiences without us knowing that it's happening.

Another study showed that if you subliminally present positively or negatively charged words while asking people to evaluate paintings and portraits, they liked or disliked the paintings respectively. Positive words like "happy" or negative words like "lazy," mild or brutal, spoken so rapidly that they went unnoticed, influenced the evaluations [52]. This indicates that when we make decisions that slow us down, or take a longer time to get to our goals, we must suspect that subliminal primes are influencing the speed at which we are reaching our goals. That is why being in a creative environment matters, and surrounding yourself with people who feel positive about their lives matters.

Control of our thinking occurs at both a conscious and unconscious level [53]. In fact, we generally overestimate the amount of control we actually have over our actions [54].

The strong influence of the unconscious on our actions suggests that even when the law of attraction appears to be not working, there are subliminal triggers or primes that may be influencing the way we act. Here are some hypothetical possibilities that illustrate this effect:

Goal that is not being reached	Possible unconscious primes
You are constantly disappointed in relationships because you end up being abandoned.	When you enter a relationship, the predominant word that comes to your consciousness is "abandoned."
You are not able to increase your income.	You are powerfully influenced by having heard "the higher you climb, the harder you fall."
You are depressed and unable to live freely without worries.	Worrying is a way of being in control; a fall while ice-skating that you experienced as a child is a nightmare of losing control.

When you are not getting what your efforts seem to indicate you should be getting, you may need to address the unconscious habits of your brain.

The Solutions

For each of your goals, if you can identify three negative early-life primes and three negative ideas that you currently hold, you can reframe these ideas.

Exercises

1. For each of your goals designated earlier, write down three possible past negative primes and then reframe them.

Goal 1:

....

....

....

Three past primes (e.g. a disappointment in the past that set you back):

....

....

....

....

....

....

Three past primes reframed (e.g. how you will use your learning from that disappointment to do something differently):

....
....
....
....
....
....

Goal 2:

....
....
....

Three past primes:

....
....
....
....
....
....

Three past primes reframed:

....
....
....

....

....

....

Goal 3:

....

....

....

Three past primes:

....

....

....

....

....

....

Three past primes reframed:

....

....

....

....

....

....

....

2. Practice these reframes for 6 weeks. Check below when you have sincerely practiced the reframe.

	Week 1	Week 2	Week 3	Week 4	Week 5	Week 6	Week 7
Yes							
No							

3. Identify three current primes that may be preventing you from reaching your goals and then reframe each of these for each goal.

Goal 1:

....

....

....

Three current primes (e.g. what else around you is stuck):

....

....

....

....

....

....

....

....

Three current primes reframed (e.g. how you will
differentiate yourself from the stuckness of all else
around you):

....

....

....

....

....

....

....

Goal 2:

....

....

....

Three current primes:

....

....

....

....

....

....

Three current primes reframed:

....

....

....

....

....

....

....

Goal 3:

....

....

....

Three current primes:

....

....

....

....

....

....

....

Three current primes reframed:

....

....

....

....

....

....

....

4. Practice these reframes for six weeks.

	Week 1	Week 2	Week 3	Week 4	Week 5	Week 6	Week 7
Yes							
No							

Law # 7

Ronco-matic intentions accelerate the brain's action plan

The Science

There are two kinds of intentions: goal intentions and implementation intentions [55]. Goal intentions refer to broad ambitions, whereas implementation intentions refer to intentions to act [56]. Implementation intentions mean that a person has decided how the plan will go into action. For example, a goal intention may be to be happier. An implementation intention derived from this would be to develop a library of mirrors (such as in Law #5) for six weeks every morning and to practice this so as to retrain your brain.

Implementation intentions have to do with the what, where, and how of things. Many people stay in the goal-intention phase because the implementation phase is too intimidating or laborious; or because while they desire a change, they dread the unknown consequences. They may even fear their own success!

There are two types of implementation intentions: promotion and prevention. For example, if you wanted to reduce unhealthy snacking, you might eat healthier snacks (promotion) or avoid unhealthy snacks (prevention). A recent study showed that if you often eat unhealthy snacks, your motivation to stop doing this would increase only if you used the implementation style that suited you [57]. That is, people have basic personality traits (they may find it easier to pursue healthy snacks rather than to avoid unhealthy snacks or vice versa), and their success in reducing unhealthy snacking depends on matching this underlying trait to their strategies. For you, then, it would be helpful to know if you find it easier to promote a healthy habit or prevent an unhealthy habit and then act accordingly.

Implementation intentions have also been shown to be effective in reducing social anxiety [58], reducing fearful reactions [59], reducing prejudice [60], eating more fruits and vegetables [61], doing more regular physical exercise [62], and walking more during one's leisure time [63]. In fact, text-messaging yourself a reminder also helps you increase physical exercise even more [64].

The simplest forms of implementation intentions are constructed as "if-then" statements. For example, if it is lunchtime on weekdays, "I will walk briskly for 20 minutes" or "I will order a low-fat meal" rather than "I intend to lose weight." This kind of specificity in self-talk can be very helpful in allowing our brains to bring us to action more easily. The "attraction" underlying this relates to the fact that our goals are more likely to be achieved when we talk to ourselves this way. We attract what we put out. If we put out vague messages to ourselves, we get less success than if we deliver specific messages to ourselves. Also, goal intentions require a self-initiated action whereas implementation intentions are previously cued and learned. While they still require us to do something ourselves, the brain thinks of them as established laws and brings us more effectively to our goals. In fact, a recent study has shown that goal intentions require more extensive brain processing in the attentional networks of the brain, and that if one specific brain region (the left lateral frontopolar cortex) is activated more, less goal achievement results [65].

Implementation intentions are more successful, not because of the deliberateness of the goal-setting per se, but actually because implementation intentions make a strong automatic link between the different parts of the intention [66]. I therefore call these "Ronco-matic" intentions— named after the "set and forget" principles of the widely advertised Ronco rotisseries.

Therefore, in order for us to attract what we want to ourselves, we have to seek to make different automatic responses. How we frame messages to ourselves matters, and we must be mindful of this as we focus on achieving our goals.

The Solutions

The basic solution here is to resolve all goal intentions into simple implementation intentions. For example, if your goal is to lose weight, rather than simply stating, "I must go to the gym three times a week and avoid unhealthy snacking," choose three situations where your goal might be challenged and reframe this as an if-then situation. For example, "If I go to a restaurant, I will order a low-fat meal" or "When I take a lunch break, I will walk briskly for the last 20 minutes." If you cannot come up with appropriate actions immediately, wrack your brain until you do. Use "The Ronco-matic Principle" (set it and forget it). Research tells us that it works. Remember that at this point, you should not merely be writing when you are writing in this workbook. This is not just an effort exercise. You will maximize your chances of getting your unconscious brain to figure out the solutions if you tell it what to do through the other six laws above. Imagine with your full body when you are breaking down goal intentions into implementation intentions.

Exercises

Refer to each of your three goals above. Now resolve all goal intentions into implementation intentions, recognizing that you are changing your brain as you do this.

Goal 1:
Goal Intention:

....
....
....

Implementation (Ronco-matic) intentions:
(1)

....
....
....

(2)

....

....

....

(3)

....

....

....

Goal 2:

Goal Intention:

....

....

....

Implementation (Ronco-matic) intentions:

(1)

....

....

....

(2)

....

....

....

(3)

....
....
....

Goal 3:

Goal Intention:

....
....
....

Implementation (Ronco-matic) intentions:

(1)

....
....
....

(2)

....
....
....

(3)

....

....

....

Conclusion

The following seven brain laws underlie the law of
attraction. You can focus on and obey them when trying
to reach your goals:

LAW	
LAW #1	The unconscious brain does the opposite of what you want it to do if you tell it not to do something.
LAW #2	Imagining what you want warms up the action center of your brain— it creates a blueprint for your action brain.
LAW #3	First- and third-person imagining activate the brain differently; embodied imagery is more effective.
LAW #4	Reframing the seemingly impossible clears the brain pathways for action.
LAW #5	The brain is geared such that we attract what we put out due to automatic mirror neurons in others.
LAW #6	Most outcomes that we attract occur due to unconscious processes, not what we consciously think.
LAW #7	The law of attraction works faster from implementation (Ronco-matic) intentions in the brain rather than goal intentions.

Each of these laws can be optimized in the brain by
doing the exercises that have been delineated in these
pages. By focusing on these research-based exercises,
you can be more certain that you are wiring your brain
to engage in the law of attraction. The idea that you get

in life what you put out is more complex than just writing a check and hoping for the best. Faith in the law of attraction is important, but to truly engage this law, you have to act into your faith.

The key to success with the law of attraction is repetition. Although the exercises in this workbook generally point to a six-week timeframe, consider this a start. Practice these exercises for a year and you will increase your chances of automatic success. If you find yourself discouraged by this timeline, recognize that it is the best way to avoid simply engaging in a fad with lack of results. Even magnets come in different strengths, and our goal here is to make your magnet the strongest magnet that it can be— one that lasts!

Bibliography

1. Wegner, D.M., *How to think, say, or do precisely the worst thing for any occasion.* Science, 2009. **325**(5936): pp. 48–50.

2. Najmi, S., et al., *Learning the futility of the thought suppression enterprise in normal experience and in obsessive compulsive disorder.* Behav Cogn Psychother, 2010. **38**(1): pp. 1–14.

3. Wegner, D.M., and R.E. Erber, *The hyperaccessibility of suppressed thoughts.* J. Pers. Soc. Psychol., 1992: p. 903.

4. Wegner, D.M., R. Erber, and S. Zanakos, *Ironic processes in the mental control of mood and mood-related thought.* J Pers Soc Psychol, 1993. **65**(6): pp. 1093–104.

5. Wegner, D.M., J.D. Lane, and J. Dimitri, *The allure of secret relationships.* Journal of Personality and Social Psychology, 1994. **66**: p. 287.

6. Wegner, D.M., and D.B. Gold, *Fanning old flames: emotional and cognitive effects of suppressing thoughts of a past relationship.* J Pers Soc Psychol, 1995. **68**(5): pp. 782–92.

7. Lebon, F., C. Collet, and A. Guillot, *Benefits of motor imagery training on muscle strength.* J Strength Cond Res, 2010. 24(6): pp. 1680–87.

8. Guillot, A., C. Tolleron, and C. Collet, *Does motor imagery enhance stretching and flexibility?* J Sports Sci, 2010. 28(3): pp. 291–98.

9. Levy, A.R., A.R. Nicholls, and R.C. Polman, *Pre-competitive confidence, coping, and subjective performance in sport.* Scand J Med Sci Sports, 2010.

10. Heremans, E., W.F. Helsen, and P. Feys, *The eyes as a mirror of our thoughts: quantification of motor imagery of goal-directed movements through eye movement registration.* Behav Brain Res, 2008. 187(2): pp. 351–60.

11. Gao, Q., X. Duan, and H. Chen, *Evaluation of effective connectivity of motor areas during motor imagery and execution using conditional Granger causality.* Neuroimage, 2010.

12. Willems, R.M., et al., *Neural dissociations between action verb understanding and motor imagery.* J Cogn Neurosci, 2010. 22(10): pp. 2387–400.

13. Munzert, J., and K. Zentgraf, *Motor imagery and its implications for understanding the motor system.* Prog Brain Res, 2009. 174: pp. 219–29.

14. Zentgraf, K., et al., *How are actions physically implemented?* Prog Brain Res, 2009. 174: pp. 303–18.

15. Decety, J., M. Jeannerod, and C. Prablanc, *The timing of mentally represented actions.* Behav Brain Res, 1989. 34(1-2): pp. 35–42.

16. Johnson, S.H., *Imagining the impossible: intact motor representations in hemiplegics.* Neuroreport, 2000. 11(4): pp. 729–32.

17. Johnson, S.H., *Thinking ahead: the case for motor imagery in prospective judgements of prehension.* Cognition, 2000. 74(1): pp. 33–70.

18. de Lange, F.P., R.C. Helmich, and I. Toni, *Posture influences motor imagery: an fMRI study.* Neuroimage, 2006. 33(2): pp. 609–17.

19. Lorey, B., et al., *The embodied nature of motor imagery: the influence of posture and perspective.* Exp Brain Res, 2009. 194(2): pp. 233–43.

20. Jeannerod, M., *The representing brain: neural correlates of motor intention and imagery.* . Behav Brain Sci, 1994. **17**: pp. 187–245.

21. Iseki, K., et al., *Neural mechanisms involved in mental imagery and observation of gait.* Neuroimage, 2008. **41**(3): pp. 1021–31.

22. Fourkas, A.D., et al., *Corticospinal facilitation during first and third person imagery.* Exp Brain Res, 2006. **168**(1-2): pp. 143–51.

23. White, A., and L. Hardy, *Use of different imagery perspectives on the learning and performance of different motor skills.* Br J Psychol, 1995. **86** (Pt 2): pp. 169–80.

24. Patuzzo, S., A. Fiaschi, and P. Manganotti, *Modulation of motor cortex excitability in the left hemisphere during action observation: a single- and paired-pulse transcranial magnetic stimulation study of self- and non-self-action observation.* Neuropsychologia, 2003. **41**(9): pp. 1272–78.

25. Hari, R., et al., *Activation of human primary motor cortex during action observation: a neuromagnetic study.* Proc Natl Acad Sci USA, 1998. **95**(25): pp. 15061–65.

26. Vealey, R.S., *Imagery training for performance enhancement.* Applied sport psychology: personal growth to peak performance, ed. J.M. Williams. 1986, Mountain View, California: Mayfield Publishing.

27. Olivetti Belardinelli, M., et al., *An fMRI investigation on image generation in different sensory modalities: the influence of vividness.* Acta Psychol (Amst), 2009. **132**(2): pp. 190–200.

28. Ertelt, D., et al., *Action observation has a positive impact on rehabilitation of motor deficits after stroke.* Neuroimage, 2007. **36** Suppl 2: pp. T164–73.

29. Buccino, G., et al., *Neural circuits involved in the recognition of actions performed by nonconspecifics: an FMRI study.* J Cogn Neurosci, 2004. **16**(1): pp. 114–26.

30. Avenanti, A., et al., *Somatic and motor components of action simulation.* Curr Biol, 2007. **17**(24): pp. 2129–35.

31. Bufalari, I., et al., *Motor imagery beyond the joint limits: a transcranial magnetic stimulation study.* Biol Psychol, 2010. **85**(2): pp. 283–90.

32. Rizzolatti, G., and C. Sinigaglia, *Mirror neurons and motor intentionality.* Funct Neurol, 2007. 22(4): pp. 205–10.

33. Rizzolatti, G., and C. Sinigaglia, *The functional role of the parieto-frontal mirror circuit: interpretations and misinterpretations.* Nat Rev Neurosci, 2010. 11(4): pp. 264–74.

34. Neal, A., and J.M. Kilner, *What is simulated in the action observation network when we observe actions?* Eur J Neurosci, 2010. 32(10): pp. 1765–70.

35. Iacoboni, M., et al., *Grasping the intentions of others with one's own mirror neuron system.* PLoS Biol, 2005. 3(3): p. e79.

36. Gallese, V., *Intentional attunement: a neurophysiological perspective on social cognition and its disruption in autism.* Brain Res, 2006. 1079(1): pp. 15–24.

37. Ramachandra, V., *On whether mirror neurons play a significant role in processing affective prosody.* Percept Mot Skills, 2009. 108(1): pp. 30–36.

38. Ramachandra, V., N. Depalma, and S. Lisiewski, *The role of mirror neurons in*

processing vocal emotions: evidence from psychophysiological data. Int J Neurosci, 2009. **119**(5): pp. 681–90.

39. Rahko, J., et al., *Functional mapping of dynamic happy and fearful facial expression processing in adolescents.* Brain Imaging Behav, 2010. 4(2): pp. 164–76.

40. Whalen, P.J., et al., *Human amygdala responsivity to masked fearful eye whites.* Science, 2004. **306**(5704): p. 2061.

41. Whalen, P.J., et al., *Masked presentations of emotional facial expressions modulate amygdala activity without explicit knowledge.* J Neurosci, 1998. **18**(1): pp. 411–18.

42. Whalen, P.J., et al., *A functional MRI study of human amygdala responses to facial expressions of fear versus anger.* Emotion, 2001. **1**(1): pp. 70–83.

43. Bishop, S.J., *Neural mechanisms underlying selective attention to threat.* Ann NY Acad Sci, 2008. **1129**: pp. 141–52.

44. Gamer, M., and C. Buchel, *Amygdala activation predicts gaze toward fearful eyes.* J Neurosci, 2009. **29**(28): pp. 9123–26.

45. Bishop, S.J., *Neurocognitive mechanisms of anxiety: an integrative account.* Trends Cogn Sci, 2007. **11**(7): pp. 307–16.

46. Schienle, A., et al., *Worry tendencies predict brain activation during aversive imagery.* Neurosci Lett, 2009. **461**(3): pp. 289–92.

47. Bramesfeld, K.D., and K. Gasper, *Happily putting the pieces together: a test of two explanations for the effects of mood on group-level information processing.* Br J Soc Psychol, 2008. **47**(Pt 2): pp. 285–309.

48. Lyubomirsky, S., L. King, and E. Diener, *The benefits of frequent positive affect: does happiness lead to success?* Psychol Bull, 2005. **131**(6): pp. 803–55.

49. Lee, S., R.D. Rogge, and H.T. Reis, *Assessing the seeds of relationship decay: using implicit evaluations to detect the early stages of disillusionment.* Psychol Sci, 2010. **21**(6): pp. 857–64.

50. Murray, S.L., J.G. Holmes, and R.T. Pinkus, *A Smart Unconscious? Procedural Origins of Automatic Partner Attitudes in Marriage.* J Exp Soc Psychol, 2010. **46**(4): pp. 650–56.

51. Gillath, O., et al., *Attachment, authenticity, and honesty: dispositional and experimentally induced security can reduce self- and other-deception.* J Pers Soc Psychol, 2010. 98(5): pp. 841–55.

52. Gibbons, H., *Evaluative priming from subliminal emotional words: insights from event-related potentials and individual differences related to anxiety.* Conscious Cogn, 2009. 18(2): pp. 383–400.

53. Lau, H.C., and R.E. Passingham, *Unconscious activation of the cognitive control system in the human prefrontal cortex.* J Neurosci, 2007. 27(21): pp. 5805–11.

54. Linser, K., and T. Goschke, *Unconscious modulation of the conscious experience of voluntary control.* Cognition, 2007. 104(3): pp. 459–75.

55. Gollwitzer, P.M., and B. Schaal, *Metacognition in action: the importance of implementation intentions.* Pers Soc Psychol Rev, 1998. 2(2): pp. 124–36.

56. Webb, T.L., P. Sheeran, and J. Pepper, *Gaining control over responses to implicit attitude tests:*

Implementation intentions engender fast responses on attitude-incongruent trials. Br J Soc Psychol, 2010.

57. Tam, L., R.P. Bagozzi, and J. Spanjol, *When planning is not enough: the self-regulatory effect of implementation intentions on changing snacking habits.* Health Psychol, 2010. 29(3): pp. 284–92.

58. Webb, T.L., et al., *Using implementation intentions to overcome the effects of social anxiety on attention and appraisals of performance.* Pers Soc Psychol Bull, 2010. 36(5): pp. 612–27.

59. Gallo, I.S., et al., *Strategic automation of emotion regulation.* J Pers Soc Psychol, 2009. 96(1): pp. 11–31.

60. Mendoza, S.A., P.M. Gollwitzer, and D.M. Amodio, *Reducing the expression of implicit stereotypes: reflexive control through implementation intentions.* Pers Soc Psychol Bull, 2010. 36(4): pp. 512–23.

61. Chapman, J., C.J. Armitage, and P. Norman, *Comparing implementation intention interventions in relation to young adults' intake*

of fruit and vegetables. Psychol Health, 2009. 24(3): pp. 317–32.

62.   Christiansen, S., et al., *A short goal-pursuit intervention to improve physical capacity: a randomized clinical trial in chronic back pain patients.* Pain, 2010. 149(3): pp. 444–52.

63.   Arbour, K.P., and K.A. Martin Ginis, *A randomised controlled trial of the effects of implementation intentions on women's walking behaviour.* Psychol Health, 2009. 24(1): pp. 49–65.

64.   Prestwich, A., M. Perugini, and R. Hurling, *Can implementation intentions and text messages promote brisk walking? A randomized trial.* Health Psychol, 2010. 29(1): pp. 40–49.

65.   Gilbert, S.J., et al., *Separable brain systems supporting cued versus self-initiated realization of delayed intentions.* J Exp Psychol Learn Mem Cogn, 2009. 35(4): pp. 905–15.

66.   Webb, T.L., and P. Sheeran, *Mechanisms of implementation intention effects: the role of goal intentions, self-efficacy, and accessibility of plan components.* Br J Soc Psychol, 2008. 47(Pt 3): pp. 373–95.

33104443R00069

Made in the USA
San Bernardino, CA
24 April 2016